Happy Birthday
Therapy

Happy Birthday Therapy

written by
Lisa Engelhardt

illustrated by
R.W. Alley

ONE
CARING
PLACE
Abbey Press

Text © 1993 Lisa Engelhardt
Illustrations © 1993 St. Meinrad Archabbey
Published by One Caring Place
Abbey Press
St. Meinrad, Indiana 47577

Library of Congress Catalog Number
93-71213

ISBN 0-87029-260-9

Printed in the United States of America

Foreword

A birthday is a milestone calling for a celebration. It means getting gifts, gathering with friends, being treated or treating ourselves. So why would anyone need "therapy" on such a joyous occasion?

Because the reality is that birthdays aren't always a wonderful "treat." A certain melancholy often surrounds them. Especially at the turn of a decade or another significant life passage, birthdays soberly remind us of unfinished business, how far we still have to go, how little time we have left to be and do what we want. They also starkly confront us with the facts of aging. Cards we receive wisecrack about skin sagging and energy diminishing as candles on the cake increase. And if there are no cards, if no one notices, we feel forgotten—even when we're not sure *we* ourselves want to remember the day!

Happy Birthday Therapy goes beyond clichés to suggest ways to use your birthday for reflection, self-affirmation, and growth. It helps you to acknowledge disappointments and regrets while appreciating how far you've come and all you have to look forward to. And its profound, life-giving message invites you to a *real* celebration of the specially ordained day when the Author of Life wrote you into history!

1.

It's your birthday—the day on which God ordained your unique place and purpose in the universe. Celebrate your beginning, your being, your becoming!

2.

Consider yourself surrounded by a radiance that proclaims: This is my special day and I am special. Then carry that feeling, that aura, with you _every_ day.

3.

Don't ignore your birthday. A birthday is a wonderful opportunity for renewing, rejuvenating, rejoicing!

4.

Remember: You belong to God. From the first moment of your existence, God's name was written in your heart. God claimed you from all eternity to be born this day, this time, into this set of circumstances.

5.

Recall what you know about your birth; find out more if you can. Reflect prayerfully on this.

6.

No matter what circumstances surrounded your birth or how it was greeted, re-image it with loved ones encircling you, welcoming you into the world, expressing joy at your arrival, delighting in the fact that you are a girl, that you are a boy.

7.

Read God's personal birthday greetings to you in the kindness of loved ones, the wonder of nature, the goodness within your heart. God's wish for you is always to feel the nearness of Grace, within and without.

8.

If you want people to remember your birthday, remind them. If you want a party and no one has planned it, throw one yourself.

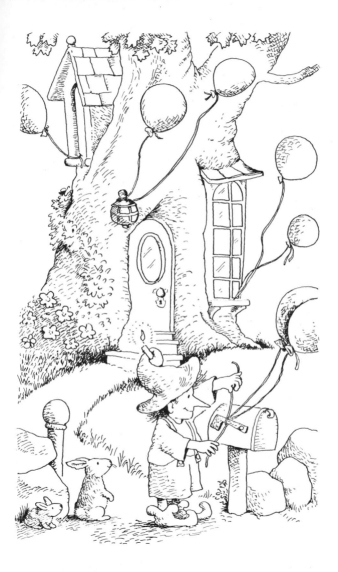

9.

Gather those you love at your hearth or in your heart. Measure your relationships not by gifts that increase your possessions but by gifts that enrich your heart: loyalty, thoughtfulness, caring, burden-sharing.

10.

Claim your birthright of joy by doing the things that you love best. Lose yourself in the fun and freedom of play. Laugh alone and with others.

11.

Count a blessing for every candle on your cake. Celebrate the abundance of your life.

12.

If you want to be alone, celebrate in solitude. The peace of coming home to your self and to God is a wonderful birthday present.

13.

If you feel an emptiness inside, don't try to stuff it with forced merrymaking. Tend first to the hole in your soul, letting God help you explore the unanswered yearnings of your heart.

14.

Celebrate the cycles of your life—the bringing forth, the flowering in fullness, the pruning back, the lying dormant. Give yourself gracefully to the season of <u>now</u>.

15.

Have a personal ritual to mark your birthday every year—for instance, say a special prayer, read a special poem, listen to special music. As the years go by, consider how the meaning of that prayer, poem, or music has changed and deepened for you.

16.

Keep a birthday journal. Each year on your birthday, write down where you are in your life's journey, how you've changed in the past year, what you've learned, how your life has been enriched.

17.

Open the scrapbook of your heart
and savor the special times
collected there. Memory gives
immortality to cherished
moments from the past.

18.

How old do you feel on the inside? Reflect on what your answer reveals about you. Celebrate the child within you—your enthusiasm, passion, hope. Celebrate the adult within you—your maturity, compassion, wisdom.

19.

Let the passage of time remind you to live mindfully and passionately. Plunge into the infinity of every moment.

20.

Send a thank you card to someone who has influenced your life in a significant way. Gratitude blesses both the receiver and the giver.

21.

If you don't like the way your body has changed since last year, consider whether you need to change your lifestyle, your clothing style, or your attitudinal style. Be nice to your body; it is the shrine of your spirit.

22.

Declare your birthday an amnesty day for anyone who has hurt you in the past year—including y<u>ou</u>. Make of your birthday a letting go—of any negativity or intolerance that distances you from your true self and from others.

23.

Write your own epitaph now—
when you don't need it—and
then start (or continue) to live
it. There's no time like a
birthday to think about who and
how you want to be.

24.

If you are discouraged at this point in your life because you don't have all the answers, be at peace. Life is not a puzzle to solve but a mystery to explore. Live the questions; love the quest.

25.

Wishes-come-true are not bestowed by some magical power. Wishes are of your own creating and your own fulfilling. Plan ahead for what you want to happen and where you want to be on your next birthday. Plans make wishes happen.

HOW
TO
POT

VOL. II

CLAY

26.

If you have regrets over paths not taken or promises to yourself not kept, think about what is keeping you from happiness right now. Give yourself what you need to change the things you can.

27.

If you feel frustrated because you are powerless over certain unwanted circumstances that have not changed since last year, draw on the Power that can manage what you can't. Pray frequently throughout the day: "Let me…let You…lead me."

28.

If this day reminds you that you are not able to fulfill your life dream, take time to bury your dream and grieve your loss. Tend the burial ground, for from it will spring the tender shoots of a new dream.

29.

If your life dream has been fulfilled, you may feel that something is still missing. Recast your dream so that it fits who you are now. Embrace your transformed dream.

30.

Don't burden yourself with impossible or unrealistic resolutions for self-improvement. Be gentle and patient with yourself. Decide that you want to do better and then let God provide the will and the way.

31.

You are a different person than you were a year ago—or even an instant ago. Be open to the fresh insight and adventure of each moment. Continually give yourself the gift of rebirth.

32.

The person you are today is a prism reflecting a unique spectrum of heredity, heritage, upbringing, and personal choices. Show your true colors with pride!

33.

You are created in love, guided by love, sustained by love. Give glory to your Creator: love yourself!

34.

You are quite literally God's gift to the world. Thank God for the gift of you by being yourself every moment of every day.

35.

Each birthday is one step higher up the mountain. Behold the view that becomes clearer and more expansive as you climb, that continually unfolds more and more of its glory before you!

36.

Happy Birthday!

Lisa O. Engelhardt is editorial director for One Caring Place/Publications at Abbey Press and the author of *Finding the Serenity of Acceptance, Acceptance Therapy*, and *Anger Therapy*. She lives with her husband and three children in Lawrenceburg, Indiana.

Illustrator for the Abbey Press Elf-help Books, **R.W. Alley** also illustrates and writes children's books. He lives in Barrington, Rhode Island, with his wife, daughter, and son.

The Story of the Abbey Press Elves

The engaging figures that populate the Abbey Press "elf-help" line of publications and products first appeared in 1987 on the pages of a small self-help book called *Be-good-to-yourself Therapy*. Shaped by the publishing staff's vision and defined in R.W. Alley's inventive illustrations, they lived out author Cherry Hartman's gentle, self-nurturing advice with charm, poignancy, and humor.

Reader response was so enthusiastic that more Elf-help Books were soon under way, a still-growing series that has inspired a line of related gift products.

The especially endearing character featured in the early books— sporting a cap with a mood-changing candle in its peak—has since been joined by a spirited female elf with flowers in her hair.

These two exuberant, sensitive, resourceful, kindhearted, lovable sprites, along with their lively elfin community, reveal what's truly important as they offer messages of joy and wonder, playfulness and co-creation, wholeness and serenity, the miracle of life and the mystery of God's love.

With wisdom and whimsy, these little creatures with long noses demonstrate the elf-help way to a rich and fulfilling life.

Elf-help Books

...adding "a little character" and a lot
of help to self-help reading!

Gratitude Therapy
#20105 $4.95   ISBN 0-87029-332-X

Garden Therapy
#20116 $4.95   ISBN 0-87029-325-7

Elf-help for Busy Moms
#20117 $4.95   ISBN 0-87029-324-9

Trust-in-God Therapy
#20119 $4.95   ISBN 0-87029-322-2

Elf-help for Overcoming Depression
#20134 $4.95   ISBN 0-87029-315-X

New Baby Therapy
#20140 $4.95   ISBN 0-87029-307-9

Grief Therapy for Men
#20141 $4.95   ISBN 0-87029-306-0

Living From Your Soul
#20146 $4.95   ISBN 0-87029-303-6

Teacher Therapy
#20145 $4.95   ISBN 0-87029-302-8

Be-good-to-your-family Therapy
#20154 $4.95   ISBN 0-87029-300-1

Stress Therapy
#20153 $4.95   ISBN 0-87029-301-X

Making-sense-out-of-suffering Therapy
#20156 $4.95   ISBN 0-87029-296-X